Table of Contents

Time Line

1774
born

John Chapman was born
in Massachusetts in 1774.
John liked to walk and
play in the woods.

◀ Massachusetts woods

Time Line

| 1774 | around 1794 |
| born | travels west |

John wanted to see
the frontier and help the
settlers. Around 1794,
John left his home. He
started walking west.

Time Line

1774
born

around 1794
travels west

1797
settles in Pennsylvania

In 1797, John settled in Pennsylvania. He collected apple seeds from nearby cider mills.

◄ pressing apples to make cider, 1800s

Time Line

1774
born

around 1794
travels west

1797
settles in Pennsylvania

John knew that apples were a good food that would last through the long winter. He planted the apple seeds. Apple trees began to grow on his land.

Time Line

| 1774 born | around 1794 travels west | 1797 settles in Pennsylvania |

John dug up some of
the young apple trees.
He planted new orchards
with them.

Time Line

1774
born

around 1794
travels west

1797
settles in Pennsylvania

In the early 1800s, John moved west again. He moved to Ohio. He sold or gave apple seeds and trees to many settlers there.

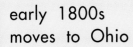 picking apples, 1800s

early 1800s
moves to Ohio

Time Line

1774
born

around 1794
travels west

1797
settles in Pennsylvania

16

John liked to read books.
Sometimes he read to
the settlers. Other times
he told stories about
himself and his apples.

◀ Johnny Appleseed (on floor) reading to settlers

early 1800s
moves to Ohio

Time Line

1774
born

around 1794
travels west

1797
settles in Pennsylvania

In 1838, John moved to Indiana. He sold apple seeds and trees to the settlers. He helped the settlers plant orchards.

Johnny Appleseed planting an orchard

early 1800s
moves to Ohio

1838
moves to Indiana

"JOHNNY APPLESEED"
JOHN CHAPMAN
HE LIVED FOR OTHERS

HOLY BIBLE

1774~1845

Time Line

1774	around 1794	1797
born	travels west	settles in Pennsylvania

John shared apple seeds,
apple trees, and stories.
Settlers gave him the
nickname Johnny Appleseed.
He died in Indiana
in 1845.

◀ Johnny Appleseed's gravesite

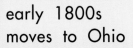
early 1800s
moves to Ohio

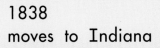
1838
moves to Indiana

1845
dies

Words to Know

cider mill—a place where fruit is pressed in order to remove its juices

frontier—the far edge of a country, where few people live

nickname—a name used instead of a person's real name; sometimes a nickname describes something about the person.

orchard—a field or farm where fruit trees are grown

settler—a person who makes a home in a new place, such as on the frontier

Read More

Harrison, David Lee. *Johnny Appleseed: My Story.* Step Into Reading. New York: Random House, 2003.

Holland, Gini. *Johnny Appleseed.* First Biographies. Austin, Texas: Raintree Steck-Vaughn, 1997.

Johnston, Marianne. *Johnny Appleseed.* American Legends. New York: PowerKids Press, 2001.

Internet Sites

Track down many sites about Johnny Appleseed. Visit the FACT HOUND at *http://www.facthound.com*

IT IS EASY! IT IS FUN!

1) Go to *http://www.facthound.com*

2) Type in: 0736816453

3) Click on "FETCH IT" and FACT HOUND will find several links hand-picked by our editors.

Relax and let our pal FACT HOUND do the research for you!

Index/Word List

Word Count: 181
Early-Intervention Level: 16

Editorial Credits

Jennifer VanVoorst, editor; Heather Kindseth, cover designer and illustrator;
   Juliette Peters, book designer; Linda Clavel, illustrator; Karrey Tweten,
   photo researcher

Photo Credits

Brand X Pictures/Bob Rashid, 4
Corbis, 1, 10; Carol Cohen, 12; Bettmann, 16
Karrey Tweten, cover
North Wind Picture Archives, 8, 14, 18
PictureQuest/Photo 24/Brand X Pictures, 6
Tom Stack & Associates/Lynn Gerig, 20